WORLD IN TRANSITION:

The 2023-2024 Political Landscape

Austin Baas

WORLD IN TRANSITION

IN THIS BOOK

1. Explore the intricate tapestry of global politics as it undergoes a transformative journey from 2023 to 2024.
2. Uncover the driving forces behind paradigm shifts, delving into economic, environmental, and technological dynamics shaping the international landscape.
3. Navigate regional complexities, from the evolving dynamics of Europe and the rise of Asia to the intricate geopolitics of the Middle East.
4. Examine the profound impact of political movements, from the surges of populism and nationalism to the influential role of social movements and activism.
5. Gain insights into the delicate dance of diplomacy and international relations, exploring the challenges and opportunities presented by shifting alliances and the evolving nature of global governance.
6. Peer into the future, as we assess the implications of these changes and uncertainties, offering a comprehensive overview of the world that awaits beyond 2024.

WORLD IN TRANSITION

TABLE OF CONTENTS

Introduction

Setting the Stage

Part I: Global Trends and Challenges

Economic Dynamics

Environmental Imperatives

Part II: Regional Shifts

Europe in Flux

Asia Rising

Middle East Reckonings

Part III: Political Movements and Upheavals

Populism and Nationalism

Social Movements and Activism

Part IV: Diplomacy and International Relations

Diplomatic Balancing Acts

Global Governance in Transition

Conclusion

Looking Ahead: The Future of Global Politics

INTRODUCTION

In the ever-evolving landscape of international relations, the years 2023 and 2024 stand as pivotal chapters in the story of our interconnected world. "World in Transition" serves as a compass, guiding readers through the turbulent waters of paradigm shifts, unveiling the profound transformations that have shaped and defined our geopolitical reality during this crucial period.

A World in Flux

In the introductory pages of this volume, we set the stage by examining the state of the world as it stood in 2023. From economic powerhouses to environmental imperatives, we delve into the multifaceted factors that laid the groundwork for the impending changes. Anticipating the unprecedented, we explore the intricate web of circumstances that propelled nations towards a nexus of decisions, choices, and challenges.

Unveiling Global Trends

The first part of the book dissects global trends and challenges that became the catalysts for seismic shifts. Economic dynamics, environmental imperatives, and technological innovations emerge as key players in the unfolding narrative. Readers are invited to witness the reshaping of trade alliances, the advent of groundbreaking technologies, and the urgent call for sustainable practices in a world grappling with climate change.

Regional Narratives

Venturing deeper, the narrative unfolds across continents, shedding light on regional shifts that redefine geopolitical landscapes. From the complexities of Europe and the rising influence of Asia to the enduring challenges of the Middle East, each chapter reveals the unique tapestry of political, cultural, and historical forces at play.

Movements and Diplomacy

Turning our focus inward, we explore the impact of political movements, examining the rise of populism, nationalism, and the transformative power of social movements and activism. Simultaneously, the book delves into the delicate intricacies of diplomacy and international relations, dissecting the ebb and flow of alliances and the evolving nature of global governance.

Looking to the Future

As we conclude this odyssey through the pages of the book, we shift our gaze forward. What does the future hold in the aftermath of these paradigm shifts? What are the key takeaways, and what uncertainties linger on the horizon? "World in Transition" offers reflections on the road ahead, providing readers with a panoramic view of the challenges and opportunities that await in the post-2024 era.

Embark on this journey with us, as we unravel the complexities of a world in transition. "World in Transition: Navigating the 2023-2024 Political Landscape" is not just a retrospective; it is a roadmap for understanding, a beacon in the fog of uncertainty, and an invitation to comprehend the intricate dance of global politics during these transformative years.

1

SETTING THE STAGE

1.1 The State of the World in 2023

In the opening chapter of our exploration into the transformative years of 2023-2024, we embark on a journey to understand the pulse of the global landscape in 2023. The geopolitical tableau, painted by the intersection of economic, social, and environmental factors, sets the stage for the impending shifts in political paradigms.

A. Economic Power Dynamics

As the world stepped into 2023, economic powerhouses found themselves at the forefront of a delicate dance. Traditional economic giants were challenged by emerging markets, and global trade patterns underwent subtle yet significant alterations. The ebb and flow of financial currents set the tone for a year where economic interdependence became both a source of strength and vulnerability.

B. Social and Cultural Crossroads

Cultures collided and converged against the backdrop of a rapidly changing world. Social movements, fueled by technological connectivity, reshaped the discourse on identity, human rights, and social justice. The echoes of societal shifts reverberated globally, challenging established norms and laying the groundwork for a new era of activism and advocacy.

C. Technological Crossroads

In the ever-accelerating race of technological advancement, the year 2023 witnessed unprecedented innovations. From artificial intelligence to renewable energy breakthroughs, the technological landscape became a key player in shaping the destiny of nations. The interplay between technology and geopolitics set the stage for a future where digital prowess would be as crucial as military might.

1.2 Anticipating Change: Factors at Play

As we delve deeper into the narrative, the anticipation of change becomes a guiding theme. Several interconnected factors played a pivotal role in shaping the geopolitical chessboard, setting the world on a course of transition.

A. Climate Imperatives

The urgent call to address climate change became a unifying force in the global agenda. Nations faced the challenge of balancing economic growth with environmental sustainability, with the specter of climate-related disasters casting a shadow over decision-makers. The quest for green policies and international cooperation on climate issues became central to the political discourse.

B. Shifting Alliances and Power Balances

The geopolitical stage witnessed a subtle yet significant recalibration of alliances. Traditional partnerships were tested, and new collaborations emerged, reflecting the evolving interests and priorities of nations. Power dynamics shifted as rising powers sought to assert their influence on the global stage, redefining the geopolitical chessboard.

C. Societal Resilience and Fragility

As the world grappled with a myriad of challenges, the resilience and fragility of societies came to the forefront. Economic disparities, political unrest, and public health crises underscored the interconnectedness of global challenges. Societal resilience became a determining factor in navigating the uncertainties of the times, while fragility exposed vulnerabilities that demanded urgent attention.

In this chapter, we lay the groundwork for a comprehensive exploration of the political landscape in the years 2023-2024. The state of the world in 2023 serves as a canvas upon which the brushstrokes of change and anticipation are painted, inviting readers to embark on a thoughtful journey through the intricacies of global transformation.

WORLD IN TRANSITION

Part I: Global Trends and Challenges

2

ECONOMIC DYNAMICS

2.1 Shifting Economic Powerhouses

The second chapter of our exploration delves into the economic dynamics that shaped the global narrative in the transformative years of 2023-2024. As we dissect the intricate web of economic forces, we witness the rise and fall of economic powerhouses, setting the stage for a new era of global economic influence.

A. Emerging Markets Take Center Stage

In the ever-evolving economic landscape, the traditional order faced challenges from the ascendancy of emerging markets. Nations once considered peripheral players emerged as economic powerhouses, reshaping the balance of economic influence. The East-West economic dichotomy blurred as regions such as Asia and Latin America showcased unprecedented growth, challenging established norms and paving the way for a more multipolar economic world.

B. The Technology Revolution in Economics

Technological advancements became a driving force behind economic transformations. The integration of artificial intelligence, blockchain, and data analytics into traditional industries disrupted existing paradigms, fostering innovation and efficiency. As nations adapted to the digital era, economic power was increasingly defined by technological prowess, giving rise to a new economic order where data became as valuable as currency.

2.2 Trade Wars and Alliances

The economic landscape of 2023-2024 was marked by the complex interplay of trade wars and alliances. Nations engaged in strategic economic maneuvers, renegotiating trade agreements and forging new alliances to safeguard their economic interests and geopolitical standing.

A. The Unfolding Trade Wars

Trade tensions, driven by protectionist policies and geopolitical rivalries, cast a shadow over the global economy. Tariffs and trade restrictions became weapons in a complex game of economic brinkmanship, with far-reaching consequences for industries and supply chains. The ripple effects of these trade wars were felt across borders, influencing economic growth, investment patterns, and the overall stability of the global market.

B. Reshaping Alliances for Economic Resilience

In response to the challenges posed by trade wars, nations sought to diversify their economic partnerships. New alliances were forged, transcending traditional geopolitical boundaries. Regional economic blocs gained prominence as nations collaborated to create resilient supply chains and reduce dependence on single markets. The economic map of the world evolved, reflecting the strategic imperatives of nations navigating the complexities of global trade.

2.3 Technological Innovations: Disruptions and Opportunities

The economic narrative of 2023-2024 was inseparable from the rapid pace of technological innovations. As breakthroughs in science and technology unfolded, they presented both disruptions and opportunities, reshaping industries and challenging traditional economic models.

A. Industry 4.0: The Fourth Industrial Revolution

The convergence of technologies such as artificial intelligence, robotics, and the Internet of Things ushered in the era of Industry 4.0. Automation and smart technologies revolutionized manufacturing processes, creating efficiencies and transforming the nature of work. Nations that embraced these technological advancements reaped the benefits of increased productivity and competitiveness, while others grappled with the social and economic implications of these transformative changes.

B. The Rise of Digital Currencies

In the economic landscape of 2023-2024, traditional notions of currency were challenged by the emergence of digital currencies. Central bank digital currencies (CBDCs) and decentralized cryptocurrencies gained prominence, posing questions about the future of monetary systems and financial transactions. The economic implications of this digital revolution extended beyond finance, influencing how nations conducted international trade and interacted within the global financial ecosystem.

As we navigate the economic dynamics of this pivotal period, it becomes clear that the forces of innovation, trade tensions, and economic realignment were instrumental in shaping the global landscape. The economic trends and challenges of 2023-2024 laid the foundation for a new economic order, setting the stage for further exploration into the multifaceted nature of global transformations.

3

ENVIRONMENTAL IMPERATIVES

3.1 Climate Change: A Global Priority

In the unfolding narrative of global dynamics during the years 2023-2024, the imperatives of the environment emerged as a central theme, transcending borders and demanding international attention. This chapter explores the urgency and impact of climate change as a driving force behind global decision-making.

A. The Climate Crisis Unveiled

As the scientific consensus on climate change solidified, the world faced the harsh reality of a planet in peril. Rising temperatures, extreme weather events, and ecological disruptions underscored the immediate need for coordinated action. Climate change became more than an environmental concern; it transformed into a complex challenge with far-reaching consequences for economies, societies, and international relations.

B. Shaping National Agendas

The recognition of climate change as a global priority reshaped national agendas across the world. Governments grappled with the dual challenge of mitigating the impacts of climate change and adapting to its inevitable consequences. Environmental considerations became integral to policy-making, influencing decisions related to energy, transportation, and infrastructure. The shift towards sustainable development became a key tenet of national strategies, reflecting a commitment to balance economic growth with ecological responsibility.

3.2 Environmental Policies and Their Impact

As nations embraced the imperative of environmental stewardship, the formulation and implementation of environmental policies became instrumental in shaping the trajectory of global sustainability.

A. Regulatory Frameworks for a Greener Future

Governments worldwide enacted ambitious environmental policies to curb emissions, protect biodiversity, and promote sustainable practices. Regulatory frameworks aimed at reducing carbon footprints, transitioning to renewable energy sources, and enforcing responsible waste management practices gained prominence. The impact of these policies rippled through industries, influencing corporate practices and reshaping the economic landscape with a renewed emphasis on eco-friendly innovation.

B. Economic Implications and Green Industries

The adoption of environmentally conscious policies brought forth a wave of economic transformation. Green industries, encompassing renewable energy, sustainable agriculture, and circular economy practices, flourished. Governments and businesses alike recognized the economic potential of embracing sustainable practices, leading to the emergence of a new economic paradigm where environmental responsibility and economic growth became mutually reinforcing objectives.

3.3 Global Initiatives for Sustainability

Collaborative efforts on the global stage became imperative to address the transnational nature of environmental challenges. This section explores international initiatives that aimed to foster global cooperation in the pursuit of sustainability.

A. United Nations Frameworks

The United Nations played a pivotal role in spearheading global initiatives for sustainability. Frameworks such as the Paris Agreement gained momentum, providing a platform for nations to collectively commit to reducing greenhouse gas emissions and limiting global temperature increases. The intersection of environmental goals with broader international development agendas marked a paradigm shift in how the world approached the interconnected challenges of climate change and sustainable development.

B. Multilateral Collaborations

Beyond the United Nations, multilateral collaborations and partnerships flourished. Nations joined forces to address cross-border environmental issues, sharing knowledge, technology, and resources. Collaborative ventures extended to research initiatives, conservation efforts, and disaster response strategies, highlighting the interconnectedness of global ecosystems and the shared responsibility of nations to safeguard the planet for future generations.

In the unfolding tapestry of global trends and challenges, environmental imperatives stand as a defining thread, weaving through the fabric of political, economic, and social landscapes. The commitment to address climate change and pursue sustainability reflects a collective acknowledgment of the need for responsible stewardship of our shared planet.

Part II: Regional Shifts

4

EUROPE IN FLUX

4.1 EU Dynamics: Unity and Discontent

As we navigate the regional shifts that marked the political landscape of 2023-2024, Europe takes center stage with a tapestry of dynamics within the European Union (EU). This chapter delves into the complexities of unity and discontent within the EU, shedding light on the internal forces shaping the continent's collective identity.

A. Unity Tested

The cohesion that defined the European Union faced unprecedented tests during this period. Internal disagreements on key issues, from economic policies to migration, strained the bonds of unity among member states. Debates over the future of the EU's political and economic integration stirred both discourse and dissent, prompting a reevaluation of the foundational principles that have guided Europe for decades.

B. The Rise of Euroscepticism

Simultaneously, a surge in Euroscepticism cast shadows on the European project. Political movements within member states questioned the benefits of EU membership, challenging the notion of a united Europe. Eurosceptic sentiments gained traction in various elections, prompting leaders to address the concerns of citizens who felt disconnected from the decision-making processes in Brussels.

4.2 Russia's Influence in Eastern Europe

The geopolitical chessboard in Eastern Europe witnessed strategic moves and counterplays, with Russia asserting its influence in the region. This section explores the nuanced dynamics of Russia's engagement with Eastern European nations during the years 2023-2024.

A. The Energy Nexus

Russia's role as a major energy supplier to Eastern Europe continued to be a focal point of geopolitical discussions. Energy agreements and disputes shaped diplomatic relations, influencing the economic and political landscapes of countries caught between energy dependence and the pursuit of diversification. The intricate dance between energy security and geopolitical interests set the stage for a complex interplay of alliances and tensions.

B. Geopolitical Maneuvering

Beyond energy, Russia's geopolitical maneuvering in Eastern Europe sought to shape regional alliances and counterbalance Western influence. Military posturing, diplomatic overtures, and information warfare played pivotal roles in defining Russia's relationships with countries in the region. The strategic chessboard in Eastern Europe became a testing ground for the balance of power between Russia and its Western counterparts.

4.3 Brexit Aftermath: UK and EU Relations

The aftermath of Brexit continued to reverberate through the corridors of power, as the United Kingdom (UK) recalibrated its relationship with the European Union. This section explores the evolving dynamics between the UK and the EU during the years 2023-2024.

A. Navigating New Norms

With the UK formally outside the EU, both entities faced the challenge of defining their relationship in the post-Brexit era. Trade agreements, regulatory frameworks, and diplomatic engagements took center stage as the UK sought to assert its newfound autonomy and the EU aimed to redefine its role on the global stage.

B. The Quest for Equilibrium

As negotiations unfolded, both the UK and the EU grappled with the complexities of finding a new equilibrium. Economic interdependence, security cooperation, and shared challenges such as climate change and public health underscored the importance of continued collaboration. The evolving dynamics between the UK and the EU became a microcosm of the broader shifts in international relations during this transformative period.

In the intricate landscape of European geopolitics, unity, external influence, and the consequences of Brexit shaped the trajectory of regional shifts. As we navigate the flux within Europe, we witness the delicate dance of nations seeking to redefine their roles in a world undergoing profound transformation.

5

ASIA RISING

5.1 China's Ascendance

In the panorama of global shifts, the rise of Asia, and particularly China, emerges as a defining force in the regional narrative. This chapter explores the multifaceted dimensions of China's ascendance and its impact on the international stage during the years 2023-2024.

A. Economic Might

China's economic prowess continued to surge, solidifying its status as a global economic powerhouse. The Belt and Road Initiative, technological advancements, and strategic investments propelled China into a leadership role in international trade and finance. As the world watched, China's economic ascendancy reshaped global supply chains and triggered a recalibration of economic relationships.

B. Geopolitical Influence

Beyond economics, China's geopolitical influence expanded. Diplomatic initiatives, strategic partnerships, and participation in international organizations underscored China's ambition to play a central role in shaping global governance. The evolving dynamics of China's relationships with other nations became a focal point, prompting discussions on cooperation, competition, and the broader implications for the international order.

5.2 Indo-Pacific Relations

The Indo-Pacific region emerged as a crucible of geopolitical dynamics, with nations navigating a complex web of alliances, rivalries, and economic interdependencies. This section delves into the evolving relations within the Indo-Pacific during the years 2023-2024.

A. Strategic Alliances

Nations in the Indo-Pacific sought to strengthen strategic alliances in response to the shifting geopolitical landscape. Security concerns, maritime disputes, and shared economic interests drove collaborations that spanned the region. The intricate dance of military partnerships and diplomatic engagements shaped the contours of power dynamics in this pivotal part of the world.

B. Economic Connectivity

Economic connectivity initiatives in the Indo-Pacific became key instruments of diplomacy. Infrastructure projects, trade agreements, and regional economic forums fostered closer economic ties. As nations jockeyed for influence, the Indo-Pacific became a theater where economic cooperation and competition intertwined, influencing not only regional stability but also the global economic order.

5.3 The Korean Peninsula: Tensions and Diplomacy

Against the backdrop of Asia's rise, the Korean Peninsula remained a focal point of geopolitical tensions and diplomatic efforts. This section examines the complex interplay of forces on the Korean Peninsula during the years 2023-2024.

A. Persistent Tensions

Tensions persisted on the Korean Peninsula, driven by historical animosities, nuclear ambitions, and military posturing. The delicate balance between North and South Korea, compounded by international concerns, created a volatile geopolitical environment. The world watched closely as events unfolded, cognizant of the potential implications for regional stability.

B. Diplomatic Initiatives

Amidst tensions, diplomatic initiatives aimed at finding a resolution gained traction. International efforts sought to bring the parties to the negotiating table, navigating a delicate path towards denuclearization and lasting peace. The Korean Peninsula became a diplomatic crucible, testing the resilience of international diplomacy in the face of longstanding regional challenges.

In the narrative of Asia rising, the ascendance of China, the intricate relations in the Indo-Pacific, and the complexities of the Korean Peninsula underscore the region's pivotal role in shaping the global landscape. As nations assert their influence and navigate regional challenges, the future trajectory of Asia becomes a crucial factor in the evolving dynamics of international relations.

6

MIDDLE EAST RECKONINGS

6.1 Shifting Alliances in the Arab World

The Middle East, perennially at the crossroads of geopolitical forces, witnessed significant shifts in alliances during the transformative years of 2023-2024. This chapter unravels the complexities of changing partnerships within the Arab world, reshaping the geopolitical landscape.

A. Diplomatic Realignment

Nations in the Arab world underwent a recalibration of diplomatic alliances, influenced by evolving regional dynamics. The emergence of new leaders, geopolitical challenges, and economic considerations prompted nations to reassess their geopolitical standing. The diplomatic chessboard in the Middle East saw new alliances forged and traditional partnerships tested, heralding a new era of geopolitical maneuvering.

6.2 Iran and the Nuclear Question

The nuclear question surrounding Iran remained a focal point of international concern, shaping regional dynamics and global diplomatic efforts. This section delves into the intricate negotiations and geopolitical implications surrounding Iran's nuclear program during the years 2023-2024.

A. Diplomacy and Distrust

International efforts to address Iran's nuclear ambitions were marked by diplomatic dialogues and periods of distrust. The delicate balance between negotiations, sanctions, and regional concerns highlighted the challenges of achieving a comprehensive and lasting agreement. The outcomes of these diplomatic endeavors held significant ramifications for regional stability and global security.

6.3 Conflict Zones: Seeking Peace in the Middle East

The quest for peace in conflict-ridden zones of the Middle East remained a pressing concern during this period. This section explores the ongoing efforts to address longstanding conflicts and foster stability in the region.

A. Israel-Palestine: Escalation and Tragedy

The Israeli-Palestinian conflict continued to escalate, with Israel's repeated attacks against Gaza and the West Bank sparking international outcry. The loss of almost 20,000 lives in mass killings brought renewed attention to the humanitarian crisis in Gaza. Israel's military actions faced criticism globally, leading to condemnations and calls for accountability. The toll on civilian populations underscored the urgency of finding a sustainable resolution to the enduring conflict.

B. Regional Impacts

The repercussions of the conflict extended beyond the immediate theater, influencing regional stability and alliances. The Middle East found itself at the intersection of geopolitical interests, with nations grappling to balance historical alliances and contemporary challenges. Efforts to seek peace and address the root causes of conflict gained renewed importance in the face of escalating tensions.

6.4 Post October 7 Scenario

A significant turning point occurred on October 7, reshaping the landscape of the Middle East and reverberating globally. This section explores the aftermath of pivotal events, examining the regional and international responses to the evolving scenario.

A. Israel's Military Setbacks

In the wake of the October 7 attacks, Israel's military faced unexpected challenges, leading to operational setbacks. The global condemnation of Israel's actions reflected a shift in international sentiment, prompting a reevaluation of alliances and diplomatic relations. The events of October 7 became a catalyst for renewed dialogue and engagement, forcing nations to confront the complexities of the Middle East's geopolitical landscape.

As we delve into the reckonings of the Middle East during 2023-2024, the shifting alliances, nuclear dilemmas, and the quest for peace underscore the intricate challenges facing the region. The echoes of conflicts and diplomatic endeavors resonate far beyond the Middle East, influencing the trajectory of global geopolitics.

Part III: Political Movements and Upheavals

7

POPULISM AND NATIONALISM

7.1 The Populist Wave

The winds of change that swept through the global political landscape during 2023-2024 carried with them a distinctive force – the populist wave. This chapter navigates the rise of populism, examining the factors that fueled its ascent and the impact it had on political dynamics worldwide.

A. The Appeal of Populism

Populist movements, characterized by their appeal to the sentiments of the ordinary citizen, gained momentum across continents. Leaders adept at harnessing public dissatisfaction with established systems and institutions found resonance among diverse populations. The populist wave became a force that challenged traditional political norms and shaped the discourse on governance and representation.

B. Economic Discontent and Social Shifts

The roots of the populist wave were embedded in economic discontent and social shifts. Inequalities, job insecurities, and cultural anxieties fueled a sense of frustration that populist leaders adeptly tapped into. The narrative of "us versus them" became a rallying cry, transcending borders and finding common ground among those who felt marginalized by the existing political order.

7.2 Nationalism's Influence on Global Politics

In tandem with the populist wave, nationalism emerged as a potent force shaping the contours of global politics. This section explores the influence of nationalism on international relations, governance, and the redefinition of national identities.

A. The Resurgence of Nationalist Sentiments

Nationalist sentiments, once considered relics of the past, experienced a resurgence during this period. Nations grappled with questions of identity, sovereignty, and the balance between global cooperation and national interests. The impact of nationalism extended beyond rhetoric, influencing policy decisions, trade relations, and the very fabric of international alliances.

B. Shifting Alliances and International Relations

Nationalism's influence on global politics manifested in the recalibration of alliances and diplomatic engagements. Nations, driven by a renewed focus on their own interests, navigated a complex landscape of shifting partnerships. The tension between national sovereignty and international collaboration became a defining feature of geopolitical interactions.

7.3 Populist Leaders: Heroes or Villains?

As populist leaders ascended to positions of power, the world grappled with the complex question of whether they were heroes championing the cause of the people or villains threatening the foundations of democracy. This section examines the personas, policies, and impacts of populist leaders on the global stage.

A. The Charisma and Controversies

Populist leaders, often charismatic and unconventional, captured the attention of their constituents and the world. However, their leadership styles were not without controversies. Policies that promised change sometimes sparked divisions, and the erosion of democratic norms raised concerns about the long-term health of democratic institutions.

B. The Global Ripple Effect

The actions of populist leaders sent ripples across borders, influencing not only domestic policies but also shaping international relations. Global institutions and alliances faced challenges as populist leaders questioned their efficacy and legitimacy. The duality of being heroes to some and villains to others underscored the divisive nature of populist movements and their impact on the global political landscape.

As we navigate the realm of populism and nationalism during the years 2023-2024, the forces of change and upheaval redefine the norms of political engagement and challenge the foundations of established order. The populist wave and the resurgence of nationalism become pivotal forces, leaving an indelible mark on the evolving narrative of global politics.

8

SOCIAL MOVEMENTS AND ACTIVISM

8.1 Youth Movements: Voices for Change

Amidst the political shifts and upheavals of 2023-2024, the voices of the youth echoed with renewed vigor, driving social movements that sought change on a global scale. This chapter explores the emergence and impact of youth movements as catalysts for social and political transformation.

A. Grassroots Mobilization

Youth movements, often rooted in grassroots activism, gained prominence as harbingers of change. From climate activism to calls for social justice, young voices mobilized to address pressing issues. The energy and passion of these movements reverberated globally, challenging established power structures and sparking a renewed sense of civic engagement.

B. Redefining Political Priorities

The narratives crafted by youth movements brought forth a redefinition of political priorities. Issues such as environmental sustainability, racial equality, and gender justice took center stage. The demands for accountability and inclusivity resonated not only within the realms of local politics but also on the international stage, shaping agendas and influencing policy discussions.

8.2 Social Media's Role in Political Activism

In the digital age, social media emerged as a powerful tool for political activism, amplifying the voices of individuals and movements. This section examines the transformative role of social media in shaping political narratives and mobilizing collective action.

A. Amplification of Activism

Social media platforms became epicenters for activism, providing individuals and movements with unprecedented reach and influence. Hashtags became rallying cries, and online campaigns facilitated the rapid dissemination of information. The viral nature of social media enabled activists to connect, organize, and mobilize on a scale previously unimaginable.

B. Challenges and Opportunities

While social media offered new avenues for political activism, it also posed challenges. The spread of misinformation, algorithmic biases, and issues of online censorship became integral to the discourse. Navigating this digital landscape required activists to adapt their strategies, harnessing the opportunities while addressing the pitfalls.

8.3 Human Rights and Global Advocacy

Against the backdrop of political movements, the advocacy for human rights took center stage, with global initiatives and campaigns seeking to address systemic injustices. This section explores the intersection of human rights and global advocacy during the transformative years of 2023-2024.

A. International Cooperation for Human Rights

Human rights became a common cause that transcended borders, prompting nations to cooperate on a global scale. International organizations, NGOs, and activists collaborated to address issues such as refugee crises, discrimination, and the protection of vulnerable populations. The interconnectedness of global challenges underscored the importance of collective action in upholding human rights.

B. Challenges to the Status Quo

Advocacy for human rights posed challenges to established power structures, prompting resistance from governments and institutions unwilling to relinquish control. The push for accountability, justice, and equality often encountered barriers, testing the resilience of global efforts to effect meaningful change.

As social movements and activism shaped the political landscape, the voices of the youth, the power of social media, and the advocacy for human rights became pivotal forces for change. In the interconnected world of 2023-2024, these movements acted as catalysts, challenging norms, inspiring action, and redefining the narrative of political engagement.

51

Part IV: Diplomacy and International Relations

9

DIPLOMATIC BALANCING ACTS

9.1 Superpower Relations: Cooperation and Competition

In the intricate dance of international relations during the transformative period of 2023-2024, the interactions between superpowers held profound implications for global stability. This chapter delves into the delicate balance of cooperation and competition that defined relations among the world's foremost nations.

A. Strategic Cooperation

Despite geopolitical tensions, superpowers engaged in strategic cooperation on issues of mutual interest. From climate change to counterterrorism, shared challenges prompted diplomatic dialogues and collaborative efforts. The dynamics of strategic partnerships became critical in navigating the complexities of an interconnected world.

B. Competition for Influence

Simultaneously, the pursuit of geopolitical influence and economic advantage fueled competition between superpowers. Strategic rivalries played out in arenas such as trade, technology, and regional influence, shaping the contours of global power dynamics. The careful navigation of these competitive landscapes became a central theme in diplomatic engagements.

9.2 Multilateralism vs. Unilateralism

The evolving nature of international relations in 2023-2024 brought forth contrasting approaches to diplomacy. This section explores the dynamics of multilateralism and unilateralism, examining how nations navigated the spectrum between collaborative frameworks and independent decision-making.

A. Multilateral Diplomacy

Nations, recognizing the complexity of global challenges, engaged in multilateral diplomacy to address shared concerns. International organizations and alliances provided platforms for collaborative decision-making, reflecting a commitment to collective solutions. The success and limitations of multilateral approaches became central to shaping diplomatic strategies.

B. Unilateral Actions

Conversely, some nations opted for unilateral actions, asserting their autonomy and pursuing independent paths. From trade policies to security decisions, unilateralism became a defining feature of certain diplomatic approaches. The implications of such actions reverberated globally, prompting debates on the efficacy and consequences of unilateral decision-making.

9.3 Diplomatic Challenges and Opportunities

The diplomatic landscape of 2023-2024 presented a myriad of challenges and opportunities that tested the acumen of nations and diplomats. This section explores the complexities that diplomats faced and the potential avenues for fostering international cooperation.

A. Cybersecurity and Information Warfare

Diplomats grappled with emerging challenges in the realm of cybersecurity and information warfare. The interconnected nature of the digital world raised concerns about the security of nations and the potential for misinformation to impact diplomatic relations. Navigating the complexities of this evolving landscape required new diplomatic strategies and international agreements.

B. Public Health and Global Cooperation

The global response to public health crises underscored the interconnectedness of nations. Diplomats faced the challenge of fostering international cooperation to address issues such as pandemics and the equitable distribution of vaccines. The collaborative efforts and shortcomings in the diplomatic response to public health crises became a testament to the need for enhanced global governance.

In the arena of diplomacy and international relations, the delicate balancing acts between superpowers, the contrasting approaches of multilateralism and unilateralism, and the myriad challenges and opportunities presented a complex tapestry. The diplomatic maneuvers of nations during 2023-2024 set the stage for the evolving dynamics of global governance and cooperation.

10

GLOBAL GOVERNANCE IN TRANSITION

10.1 United Nations: Reforms and Resilience

The United Nations (UN), as the cornerstone of global governance, underwent a period of transformation and resilience during the years 2023-2024. This chapter examines the reforms initiated within the UN and its resilience in the face of emerging challenges.

A. Institutional Reforms

Recognizing the evolving nature of global challenges, the UN embarked on institutional reforms aimed at enhancing its effectiveness. Discussions on Security Council expansion, changes in decision-making processes, and efforts to address issues of representation gained momentum. The pursuit of reforms reflected the commitment to adapt the UN to the realities of a changing world.

B. Crisis Response and Humanitarian Efforts

The UN demonstrated resilience in its crisis response and humanitarian efforts. From natural disasters to conflicts, the organization played a pivotal role in coordinating international aid and fostering cooperation among nations. The challenges posed by global crises underscored the ongoing importance of the UN in addressing collective challenges.

10.2 International Organizations: Adapting to Change

Beyond the UN, other international organizations faced the imperative to adapt to a rapidly changing geopolitical landscape. This section explores how these organizations navigated the challenges of the period and adjusted their strategies to remain relevant.

A. Regional Organizations and Collaborations

Regional organizations played an increasingly vital role in addressing regional challenges. Collaborations between regional blocs and international organizations became more pronounced, reflecting the need for nuanced approaches to diverse geopolitical contexts. The effectiveness of these collaborative efforts became a key determinant of success in addressing regional issues.

B. Economic and Trade Organizations

Economic and trade organizations faced the complexities of a shifting global economic order. Discussions on trade agreements, economic cooperation, and financial stability took center stage. The ability of these organizations to adapt to the economic realities of the time shaped their influence on global economic governance.

10.3 The Role of Non-State Actors

Non-state actors, ranging from corporations to civil society organizations, played an increasingly influential role in shaping global governance. This section examines the evolving role of non-state actors and their impact on diplomatic and international relations.

A. Corporate Diplomacy

Multinational corporations engaged in diplomatic initiatives and global governance discussions, leveraging their economic influence for social and political objectives. Corporate responsibility, sustainability, and ethical business practices became integral components of the global governance conversation.

B. Civil Society and Activism

Civil society organizations and activists, empowered by connectivity and social media, actively contributed to global governance discussions. Their advocacy for human rights, environmental sustainability, and social justice added new dimensions to diplomatic dialogues. The ability of non-state actors to influence policy agendas highlighted the evolving nature of global governance in a interconnected world.

As global governance underwent a period of transition, the resilience of international organizations, the adaptability of non-state actors, and the reforms within institutions like the United Nations shaped the contours of diplomatic engagements. The evolving dynamics reflected a collective effort to address the complexities of a rapidly changing world and foster international cooperation for the common good.

CONCLUSION

11

LOOKING AHEAD : THE FUTURE OF GLOBAL POLITICS

11.1 Key Takeaways

As we reflect on the tumultuous year of 2023 and the transformative shifts in global politics, certain key takeaways emerge. The intricate interplay of political, economic, and social forces has reshaped the world order, challenging established norms and inspiring a reevaluation of diplomatic strategies. The voices of youth, the rise of populism, and the growing influence of non-state actors have added new dimensions to the international stage. The dynamics of global governance have undergone profound shifts, with institutions like the United Nations adapting to the demands of a changing world. The future of global politics is one of complexity, uncertainty, and the potential for both challenges and opportunities.

11.2 Predictions and Uncertainties

While we can discern certain trends and patterns from the events of 2023-2024, the future of global politics remains inherently uncertain. Predicting the geopolitical landscape requires an acknowledgment of the fluid nature of international relations. The balance of power among superpowers, the trajectory of regional dynamics, and the role of emerging technologies are all factors that will influence the course of global politics. The uncertainties that lie ahead necessitate a diplomatic mindset that embraces adaptability, foresight, and a commitment to addressing the unforeseen challenges that may emerge.

11.3 The Call for Global Cooperation

Amidst the complexities and uncertainties, one resounding call echoes through the corridors of global politics: the imperative for global cooperation. The challenges of the 21st century—from climate change and public health crises to economic inequalities—are inherently transnational. Addressing these challenges requires collaborative efforts, shared responsibilities, and a commitment to the common good. The future of global politics hinges on the ability of nations to transcend geopolitical rivalries, ideological differences, and short-term interests in favor of a collective vision for a more stable, equitable, and sustainable world.

In the chapters that unfold the narrative of 2023-2024, we witness a world in flux, navigating through political paradigms, regional shifts, social movements, and diplomatic intricacies. As we look ahead, the pages of the future are unwritten, awaiting the actions and decisions of the global community. The story of global politics is an ever-evolving narrative, shaped by the choices we make, the challenges we confront, and the collaborative endeavors that define our shared journey into the unknown. The future beckons, and the responses of nations to the call for global cooperation will determine the course of history in the years to come.